SeeNoEvil

T O Z A K E   S H A N G E

SeeNoEvil

PREFACES, ESSAYS & ACCOUNTS
1976–1983

Momo's Press   1984   San Francisco

Funding for this volume was made partially
possible by a grant from the National Endowment
for the Arts, a Federal Agency. Momo's Press is a
project of the Intersection, San Francisco.

"Preface" is reprinted with permission of
Macmillan Publishing Company from *for colored
girls who have considered suicide/when the
rainbow is enuf* by Ntozake Shange.
Copyright © 1975, 1976, 1977.

"forward/unrecovered losses/black theater
traditions" is from *Three Pieces: (Spell #7, A
Photograph: Lovers in Motion, Boogie Woogie
Landscapes)* by Ntozake Shange and is reprinted
by permission of St. Martin's Press, Inc. Copyright
© 1981 by Ntozake Shange, St. Martin's Press, Inc.

Other essays, articles and reviews in this volume
were previously published variously in the *Voice,
Yardbird Reader,* and *Dance Magazine.*

**Library of Congress
Cataloging in Publication Data**

SHANGE, NTOZAKE.
See No Evil.

I. Title.
PS3569.H3324S4 1984   818'.5408   83-25083
ISBN 0-917672-22-4
ISBN 0-917672-21-6 (pbk.)

First Edition

Book design by Jon Goodchild/Triad.

Cover Photograph Copyright © 1983 by Ntozake
Shange.

Back Cover photograph of Ntozake Shange © 1984
by Gregory Gerran.

Illustrations © 1984 by Tom Feelings.

Printed in the United States of America.

Momo's Press
45 Sheridan Street,
San Francisco, CA 94103

Contents

Prologue:

worlds like words for a woman who is a poet and
a mother are confusing / overlapping contradictory
fatigue & exciting. between diapers, the park, the
telephone conversations with e.t. and the dollhouse
which had to be a plantation house where little black babies
rest and play between my poems. my incomplete thoughts.
thoughts i never find the ends of: lose threads on dresses, in
my soul there lies a quiet that sleeps out in the night
after the last bottle and the last dried dish. somewhere
between the unfinished books i am dying to read.
among the letters to friends i cant finish. there
is a quiet that booms and presses me out of my bed. out of my tiredness
and sense of complete isolation from all the rest of
you. they are here in this book. i see no evil. i am
fighting demons in the dark and the energies of a free spirit
        who must know
this world will do its best to take from her all she is unless she is
willing to struggle as she struggles with me for *the right to see*.

Ntozake Shange
12 April 1983. Houston

SeeNoEvil

A History

for colored girls who have considered suicide/ when the rainbow is enuf

for colored girls who have considered suicide/ when the rainbow is enuf was first presented at the Bacchanal, a woman's bar just outside Berkeley, California. With Paula Moss & Elvia Marta who worked with me in Raymond Sawyer's Afro-American Dance Company & Halifu's The Spirit of Dance; Nashira Ntosha, a guitarist & program coordinator at KPOO-FM (one of the few Bay Area stations focusing on women's programming); Jessica Hagedorn, a poet & reading tour companion; & Joanna Griffin, co-founder of the Bacchanal & a poet. We just did it. Working in bars waz a circumstantial aesthetic of poetry in San Francisco from Specs, an old beat hangout, to 'new' Malvina's, Minnie's Can-Do Club, the Coffee Gallery, & the Ribeltad Vorden. With as much space as a small studio on the Lower East Side, the five of us, five women, proceeded to dance, make poems, make music, make a woman's theater for about twenty patrons. This was December of 1974. We were a little raw, self-conscious, & eager. Whatever we were discovering in ourselves that nite had been in process among us for almost two years.

I first met Jessica & Nashira thru Third World Communications (The Woman's Collective) when the first anthology of Third World women writers in the U.S.A. was published. With Janice Mirikitani, Avotcja, Carol Lee Sanchez, Janet Campbell Hale, Kitty Tsui, Janice Cobb, Thulani, and a score more, San Francisco waz inundated with women poets, women's readings, & a multi-lingual woman presence, new to all of us & desperately appreciated. The force of these readings on all our lives waz to become evident as we directed our energies toward clarifying our lives—& the lives of our mothers, daughters, & grandmothers—as women. During the same period, Shameless Hussy Press & The Oakland Women's Press Collective were also reading anywhere & everywhere they could. In a single season, Susan Griffin, Judy Grahn, Barbara Gravelle, & Alta, were promoting the poetry &

presence of women in a legendary male-poet's environment. This is the energy & part of the style that nurtured *for colored girls* . . .

More stable as a source of inspiration & historical continuity waz the Women's Studies Program at Sonoma State College, where I worked with J.J. Wilson, Joanna Griffin, & Wopo Holup over a three year span. Cources designed to make women's lives & dynamics familiar to us, such as: Woman as Artist; Woman as Poet; Androgynous Myths in Literature; Women's Biography I & II; Third World Women Writers, are inextricably bound to the development of my sense of the world, myself, & women's language. Studying the mythology of women from antiquity to the present day led directly to the piece *Sechita* in which a dance hall girl is perceived as deity, as slut, as innocent & knowing. Unearthing the mislaid, forgotten, & / or misunderstood women writers, painters, mothers, cowgirls, & union leaders of our pasts proved to be both a supportive experience & a challenge not to let them down, not to do less than—at all costs not be less woman than—our mothers, from Isis to Marie Laurencin, Zora Neale Hurtson to Kathe Kollwitz, Anna May Wong to Calamity Jane.

Such joy & excitement I knew in Sonoma, then I would commute back the sixty miles to San Francisco to study dance with Raymond Sawyer, Ed Mock, & Halifu. Knowing a woman's mind & spirit had been allowed me, with dance I discovered my body more intimately than I had imagined possible. With the acceptance of the ethnicity of my thighs & backside, came a clearer understanding of my voice as a woman & as a poet. The freedom to move in space, to demand of my own sweat a perfection that could continually be approached, though never known, waz poem to me, my body & mind ellipsing, probably for the first time in my life. Just as Women's Studies had rooted me to an articulated female heritage & imperative, so dance as explicated by Raymond Sawyer & Ed Mock insisted that everything African, every-thing halfway colloquial, a grimace, a strut, an arched back over a yawn, waz mine. I moved what waz my unconsious knowledge of being in a colored woman's body to my known everydayness. The depth of my past waz made tangible to me in Sawyer's *Ananse*, a dance exploring the Diaspora to contemporary Senegalese music, pulling ancient trampled spirits out of present tense Afro-American Dance. Watching Ed Mock re-create the Step Brothers' or Bert Williams' routines in class or on stage, in black face mimicking Eddie Cantor or Gloria Swanson, being the rush of irony & control that are the foundation of jazz dance, was as startling as humbling. With Raymond Sawyer & Ed Mock, Paula Moss & I learned the wealth of our bodies, if we worked, if we opened up, if we made the dance our own.

14

The first experience of women's theater for me as a performer waz the months I spent with Halifu Osumare's The Spirit of Dance, a troupe of five to six black women who depicted the history of Black dance from its origins in Western Africa thru to the popular dances seen on our streets. Without a premeditated or conscious desire to create a female piece, that's what, in fact, Halifu did. Working in San Francisco & Berkeley public schools as an adjunct to Ethnic Studies, I learned the mechanics of self-production & absorbed some of Halifu's confidence in her work, the legitimacy of our visions. After some 73 performances with The Spirit of Dance, I left the company to begin production of *for colored girls* . . .

In the summer of 1974 I had begun a series of seven poems, modeled on Judy Grahn's *The Common Woman*, which were to explore the realities of seven different kinds of women. They were numbered pieces: the women were to be nameless & assume hegemony as dictated by the fullness of their lives. The first of the series is the poem, 'one' (orange butterflies & aqua sequins), which prompted the title *& this is for colored girls who have considered suicide / when the rainbow is enuf*. I waz smitten by my own language, & called all the performances I waz to give from then on by that title. In other words, all the readings & choreopoetry that Paula Moss & I developed after that summer waz *for colored girls*. . . . We started at the Bacchanal & worked through the winter at Ed Mock's Dance Studio with the assistance of West Coast Dance Works, setting pieces & cleaning up poems. I found two bands, The Sound Clinic (a horn trio) & Jean Desarmes & His Raggae Blues Band, who agreed to work with us if I found space. & I did. The space we used waz the space I knew: Women's Studies Departments, bars, cafes, & poetry centers. With the selection of poems changing, dependent upon our audience & our mood, & the dance growing to take space of its own, so that Paula inspired my words to fall from me with her body, & The Sound Clinic working with new arrangements of Ornette Coleman compositions & their own, The Raggae Blues Band giving Caribbean renditions of Jimi Hendrix & Redding, we set dates for Minnie's Can-Do Club in Haight-Ashbury. The poets showed up for us, the dancers showed up for us, the women's community showed up, & we were listed as a 'must see' in *The Bay Guardian*. Eight days after our last weekend at Minnie's, Paula & I left to drive cross country to New York to do 'the show,' as we called it, at the Studio Rivbea in New York.

Our work in San Francisco waz over. With the courage of children, we staged the same sort of informal & improvised choreopoems at Rivbea during the Summer Music Festival. Instead of the Standing-Room-

Only crowds we were accustomed to in San Francisco, my family & a few friends came to see our great project. One of these friends, Oz Scott, & my sister, Ifa Iyaun, who were instrumental in the development of *for colored girls* . . . saw the show that night. Oz offered to help me with the staging of the work for a New York audience, since Paula & I obviously didn't understand some things. We moved from the Rivbea to the Old Reliable on East 3rd Street to work through some of the ideas Oz had & the new things Paula & I were developing.

Gylan Kain of the Original Last Poets waz working there every Monday night. We worked with him & any other poets & dancers who showed up. Several members of the original New York show came to us just this haphazardly. Aku Kadogo & I both had scholarships at Diane McIntyre's Sounds-in-Motion Dance Studio. I asked her if she felt like improvising on the Lower East Side, she agreed & has been with the show ever since. Laurie Carlos stopped by one evening. She stayed. Somehow word got out & people started coming to the back room of this neighborhood bar. We were moved to a new bar down the street, DeMonte's, after eleven weeks of no-pay hardwork three sets a night—maybe a shot of cognac on the house.

The show at DeMonte's waz prophetic. By this time, December of 1975, we had weaned the piece of extraneous theatricality, enlisted Trazana Beverley, Laurie Carlos, Laurie Hayes, Aku Kadogo, & of course, Paula & I were right there. The most prescient change in the concept of the work waz that I gave up directorial powers to Oz Scott. By doing this, I acknowledged that the poems & the dance worked on their own to do & be what they were. As opposed to viewing the pieces as poems, I came to understand these twenty-odd poems as a single statement, a choreopoem.

We finally hit at DeMonte's. Those institutions I had shunned as a poet—producers, theaters, actresses, & sets—now were essential to us. *for colored girls who have considered suicide / when the rainbow is enuf* waz a theater piece. Woody King picked up our option to produce us as a Workshop under Equity's Showcase Code at Henry Street. With the assistance of the New York Shakespeare Festival & Joe Papp, we received space & a set, lights & a mailing list, things Paula & I had done without for two years. We opened at Henry Street with two new actress-dancers, Thea Martinez & Judy Dearing. Lines of folks & talk all over the Black & Latin community propelled us to the Public Theater in June. Then to the Booth Theater on Broadway in September of 1976.

Every move we've made since the first showing of *for colored girls . . .* in California has demanded changes of text, personnel, & staging. The final production at the Booth is as close to distilled as any of us in all our art forms can make it. With two new actresses, Janet League & Rise Collins, & with the help of Seret Scott, Michelle Shay, & Roxanne Reese, the rest of the cast is enveloping almost 6,000 people a week in the words of a young black girl's growing up, her triumphs & errors, our struggle to become all that is forbidden by our environment, all that is forfeited by our gender, all that we have forgotten.

I had never imagined not doing *for colored girls. . . .* It waz just my poems, any poems I happened to have. Now I have left the show on Broadway, to write poems, stories, plays, my dreams. *for colored girls . . .* is either too big for my off-off Broadway taste, or too little for my exaggerated sense of freedom, held over from seven years of improvised poetry readings. Or, perhaps, the series has actually finished itself. Poems come on their own time: i am offering these to you as what i've received from this world so far.

i am on the other side of the rainbow / picking up the pieces of days spent waitin for the poem to be heard / while you listen / i have other work to do /

new york, 1976

A Foreword to Three Pieces:
(Spell #7, A Photograph: Lovers in Motion, Boogie Woogie Landscapes)

Unrecovered Losses/
Black Theater Traditions

as a poet in american theater/ i find most activity that takes place on our stages overwhelmingly shallow/ stilted & imitative. that is probably one of the reasons i insist on calling myself a poet or writer/ rather than a playwright/ i am interested solely in the poetry of a moment/ the emotional & aesthetic impact of a character or a line. for too long now afro-americans in theater have been duped by the same artificial aesthetics that plague our white counterparts/ "the perfect play," as we know it to be/ a truly european framework for european psychology/ cannot function efficiently for those of us from this hemisphere.

furthermore/ with the advent of at least 6 musicals about the lives of black musicians & singers/ (EUBIE, BUBBLING BROWN SUGAR, AIN'T MISBEHAVIN', MAHALIA, etc.)/ the lives of millions of black people who dont sing & dance for a living/ are left unattended to in our theatrical literature. not that the lives of Eubie Blake or Fats Waller are well served in productions lacking any significant book/ but if the lives of our geniuses arent artfully rendered/ & the lives of our regular & precious are ignored/ we have a double loss to reckon with.

if we are drawn for a number of reasons/ to the lives & times of black people who conquered their environments/ or at least their pain with their art, & if these people are mostly musicians & singers & dancers/ then what is a writer to do to draw the most human & revealing moments from lives spent in nonverbal activity. first of all we should reconsider our choices/ we are centering ourselves around these artists for what reasons/ because their lives were richer than ours/ because they did something white people are still having a hard time duplicating/ because they proved something to the world like Jesse Owens did/ like Billie Holiday did. i think/ all the above contributes to the proliferation of musicals abt our musicians/ without forcing us to confront the real implications of the dynamic itself. we are compelled to examine these giants in order to give ourselves what

we think they gave the worlds they lived in/ which is an independently
created afro-american aesthetic. but we are going abt this process
backwards/ by isolating the art forms & assuming a very narrow per-
spective vis-à-vis our own history.

if Fats Waller & Eubie Blake & Charlie Parker & Savilla Fort &
Katherine Dunham moved the world outta their way/ how did they
do it/ certainly not by mimicking the weakest area in american art/
the american theater. we must move our theater into the drama of our
lives/ which is what the artists we keep resurrecting (or allowing
others to resurrect) did in the first place/ the music & dance of our
renowned predecessors appeals to us because it directly related to
lives of those then living & the lives of the art forms.

in other words/ we are selling ourselves & our legacy quite cheaply/
since we are trying to make our primary statements with somebody
else's life/ and somebody else's idea of what theater is. i wd suggest
that: we demolish the notion of straight theater for a decade or so,
refuse to allow playwrights to work without dancers & musicians.
"coon shows" were somebody else's idea. we have integrated the
notion that a drama must be words/ with no music & no dance/ cuz
that wd take away the seriousness of the event/ cuz we all remember
too well/ the chuckles & scoffs at the notion that all niggers cd sing &
dance/ most of us can sing & dance/ & the reason that so many plays
written to silence & stasis fail/ is cuz most black people have some
music & movement in our lives. we do sing & dance. this a cultural
reality. that is why i find the most inspiring theater among us to be in
the realms of music & dance.

i think of my collaboration with David Murray on A PHOTO-
GRAPH/ & on WHERE THE MISSISSIPPI MEETS THE AMAZON/
& on SPELL #7/ in which music functions as another character.
Teddy & his Sizzling Romancers (David Murray, sax.; Anthony Davis,
piano; Fred Hopkins, bass; Paul Maddox, drums; Michael Gregory
Jackson, guitar, harmonica & vocals) were as important as The Satin
Sisters/ though the thirties motif served as a vehicle to introduce the
dilemmas of our times. in A PHOTOGRAPH the cello (Abdul Wadud)
& synthesizer (Michael Gregory Jackson) solos/ allowed Sean to
break into parts of himself that wd have been unavailable had he been
unable to "hear." One of the bounties of black culture is our ability to
"hear"/ if we were to throw this away in search of less (just language)
we wd be damning ourselves. in slave narratives there are numerous
references to instruments/ specifically violins, fifes & flutes/
"talking" to the folks. when working with Oliver Lake (sax.) or
Baikida Carroll (tr.) in FROM OKRA TO GREENS/ or Jay Hoggard
(vibes) in FIVE NOSE RINGS & SOWETO SUITE/ i am terribly
aware of a conversation. in the company of Dianne McIntyre/ or
Dyane Harvey's work with the Eleo Pomare Dance Company/ one is

continually aroused by the immediacy of their movements/ "do this movement like yr life depends on it"/ as McIntyre says.

the fact that we are an interdisciplinary culture/ that we understand more than verbal communication/ lays a weight on afro-american writers that few others are lucky enough to have been born into. we can use with some skill virtually all our physical senses/ as writers committed to bringing the world as we remember it/ imagine it/ & know it to be to the stage/ we must use everything we've got. i suggest that everyone shd cue from Julius Hemphill's wonderful persona, Roi Boye/ who ruminates & dances/ sings & plays a saxophone/ shd cue from Cecil Taylor & Dianne McIntyre's collaboration on SHADOWS/ shd cue from Joseph Jarman & Don Moye (of the Art Ensemble of Chicago) who are able to move/ to speak/ to sing & dance & play a myriad of instruments in EGWU-ANWU. look at Malinke who is an actor/ look at Amina Myers/ Paula Moss/ Aku Kadogo/ Michelle Shay/ Laurie Carlos/ Ifa Iyaun Baeza & myself in NEGRESS/ a collective piece which allowed singers, dancers, musicians & writers to pass through the barriers & do more than 1 thing. dance to Hemphill or the B.A.G. (Black Artist Group)/ violinist Ramsey Amin lets his instrument make his body dance & my poems shout. i find that our contemporaries who are musicians are exhibiting more courage than we as writers might like to admit.

in the first version of BOOGIE WOOGIE LANDSCAPES i presented myself with the problem of having my person/ body, voice & language/ address the space as if i were a band/ a dance company & a theater group all at once. cuz a poet shd do that/ create an emotional environment/ felt architecture.

to paraphrase Lester Bowie/ on the night of the World Saxophone Quartet's (David Murray, Julius Hemphill, Hamiett Bluiett & Oliver Lake) performance at the Public Theater/ "those guys are the greatest comedy team since the Marx Brothers." in other words/ they are theater. theater which is an all encompassing moment/ a moment of poetry/ the opportunity to make something happen. We shd think of George Clinton/ a.k.a. Dr. Funkenstein/ as he sings/ "here's a chance to dance our way out of our constrictions." as writers we might think more often of the implications of an Ayler solo/ the meaning of a contraction in anybody's body. we are responsible for saying how we feel. we "ourselves" are high art. our world is honesty & primal response.

1/22/79   NYC

Program Note

    although i rarely read reviews of my work/ two comments were repeated to me by "friends" for some reason/ & now that i am writing abt my own work/ i am finally finding some use for the appraisals of strangers. one new york critic had accused me of being too self-conscious of being a writer/ the other from the midwest had asserted that i waz so involved with the destruction of the english language/ that my writing approached verbal gymnastics like unto a reverse minstrel show. in reality/ there is an element of truth in both ideas/ but the lady who thought i waz self-conscious of being a writer/ apparently waz never a blk child who knew that no black people conducted themselves like amos n andy/ she waz not a blk child who knew that blk children didnt wear tiger skins n chase lions around trees n then eat pancakes/ she waznt a blk child who spoke english that had evolved naturally/ only to hear a white man's version of blk speech that waz entirely made up & based on no linguistic system besides the language of racism. the man who thought i wrote with intentions of outdoing the white man in the acrobatic distortions of english waz absolutely correct. i cant count the number of times i have viscerally wanted to attack deform n maim the language that i waz taught to hate myself in/ the language that perpetuates the notions that cause pain to every black child as he/she learns to speak of the world & the "self." yes/ being an afro-american writer is something to be self-conscious abt/ & yes/ in order to think n communicate the thoughts n feelings i want to think n communicate/ i haveta fix my tool to my needs/ i have to take it apart to the bone/ so that the malignancies/ fall away/ leaving us space to literally create our own image.

    i have not ceased to be amazed when i hear members of an audience whispering to one another in the foyers of theaters/ that they had never imagined they cd feel so much for characters/ even though they were black (or colored/ or niggers, if they don't notice me eavesdropping). on the other hand/ i hear other members of an audience say that there were so many things in the piece that they had felt/ experienced/ but had never found words to express/ even privately/ to themselves. these two phenomena point to the same dilemma/ the straitjacket that the english language slips over the minds of all americans. there are some thoughts that black people just dont have/ according to popular mythology/ so white people never "imagine" we are having them/ & black people "block" vocabularies we perceive to be white folks' ideas.* this will never do. for in addition to the

---

*Just examine *Drylongso* by John Langston Gwaltney, Random House, 1980.

obvious stress of racism n poverty/ afro-american culture/ in attempts to carry on/ to move forward/ has minimized its "emotional" vocabulary to the extent that admitting feelings of rage, defeat, frustration is virtually impossible outside a collective voice. so we can add self-inflicted repression to the cultural causes of our cultural disease of high blood pressure.

in everything i have ever written & everything i hope to write/ i have made use of what Frantz Fannon called "combat breath." although Fanon waz referring to francophone colonies, the schema he draws is sadly familiar:

there is no occupation of territory, on the one hand, and independence of persons on the other. It is the country as a whole, its history, its daily pulsation that are contested, disfigured, in the hope of final destruction. Under this condition, the individual's breathing is an observed, an occupied breathing. It is a combat breathing. †

Fanon goes on to say that "combat breathing" is the living response/ the drive to reconcile the irreconcilable/ the black & white of what we live n where. (unfortunately, this language doesnt allow me to broaden "black" & "white" to figurative terms/ which is criminal since the words are so much larger n richer than our culture allows.) i have lived with this for 31 years/ as my people have lived with cut-off lives n limbs. the three pieces in this collection are the throes of pain n sensation experienced by my characters responding to the involuntary constrictions n amputations of their humanity/ in the context of combat breathing.

each of these pieces was excruciating to write/ for i had to confront/ again & again/ those moments that had left me with little more than fury n homicidal desires. in *spell #7* i included a prologue of a minstrel show/ which made me cry the first times i danced in it/ for the same reasons i had included it. the minstrel may be "banned" as racist/ but the minstrel is more powerful in his deformities than our alleged rejection of him/ for every night we wd be grandly applauded. immediately thereafter/ we began to unveil the "minstrels," who turned out to be as fun-loving as fay:

please/ let me join you/ i come all the way from brooklyn/ to have a good time/ ya dont think i'm high do ya/ cd i please join ya/ i just wanna have a good ol time.

as contorted as sue-jean:

---

†Frantz Fanon, *A Dying Colonialism*, Grove Press, 1967.

& i lay in the corner laughin/ with my drawers/ twisted round my ankles & my hair standin every which way/ i waz laughin/ knowin i wd have this child/ myself/ & no one wd ever claim him/ cept me/ cuz i was a low-down thing/ layin in sawdust & whiskey stains/ i laughed & had a good time masturbatin in the shadows.

as angry as the actor who confides:

i just want to find out why no one has even been able to sound a gong & all the reporters recite that the gong is ringin/ while we watch all the white people/ immigrants & invaders/ conquista-dors & relatives of london debtors from georgia/ kneel & apologize to us/ just for three or four minutes. now/ this is not impossible.

& after all that/ our true visions & rigors laid bare/ down from the ceiling comes the huge minstrel face/ laughing at all of us for having been so game/ we believed we cd escape his powers/ how naive cd we be/ the magician explains:

*crackers are born with the right to be alive/
i'm making ours up right here in yr face.*

the most frequently overheard comment abt *spell #7* when it first opened at the public theater/ waz that it waz too intense. the cast & i usedta laugh. if this one hour n 45 minutes waz too much/ how in the world did these same people imagine the rest of our lives were/ & wd they ever be able to handle that/ simply being alive & black & feeling in this strange deceitful country. which brings me to *boogie woogie landscapes/* totally devoted to the emotional topology of a yng woman/ how she got to be the way she is/ how she sees where she is. here/ again/ in the prologue lies the combat breath of layla/ but she's no all-american girl/ or is she?

the lil black things/ pulled to her & whimpered lil black whys/ 'why did those white men make red of our house/ why did those white men want to blacken even the white doors of our house/ why make fire of our trees/ & our legs/ why make fire/ why laugh at us/ say go home/ arent we home/ arent we home?'

she waz raised to know nothing but black & white two-dimensional planes/ which is what racism allots everyone of us unless we fight. she found solace in jesus & the american way/ though jonestown & american bandstand lay no claims to her:

*shall i go to jonestown or the disco? i cd wear red sequins or a
burlap bag. maybe it doesnt matter/ paradise is fulla surprises/
& the floor of the disco changes colors like special species
of vipers . . .*

her lover/ her family/ her friends torment her/ calm her with the
little they have left over from their own struggles to remain sane.
everything in *boogie woogie landscapes* is the voice of layla's uncon-
scious/ her unspeakable realities/ for no self-respecting afro-american
girl wd reveal so much of herself of her own will/ there is too much
anger to handle assuredly/ too much pain to keep on truckin/ less ya
bury it.

   both *spell #7 & boogie woogie landscapes* have elements of
magic or leaps of faith/ in typical afro-american fashion/ not only will
the lord find a way/ but there *is* a way outta here. this is the litany
from the spirituals to Jimi Hendrix' "there must be some kinda way
outta here"/ acceptance of my combat breath hasnt closed the possibilities of hope to me/ the soothing actualities of music n sorcery/
but that's why i'm doubly proud of *a photograph: lovers in motion*/
which has no cures for our "condition" save those we afford ourselves. the characters michael/ sean/ claire/ nevada/ earl/ are
afflicted with the kinds of insecurities & delusions only available to
those who learned themselves thru the traumas of racism. what is fas-
cinating is the multiplicity of individual responses to this kind of
oppression. michael displays her anger to her lovers:

*i've kept a lover who waznt all-american/ who didnt believe/
wdnt straighten up/ oh i've loved him in my own men/ sometimes hateful sometimes subtle like high fog & sun/ but who i
loved is yr not believin. i loved yr bitterness & hankered after
that space in you where you are outta control/ where you cannot touch or you wd kill me/ or somebody else who loved you. i
never even saw a picture & i've loved him all my life he is all
my insanity & anyone who loves me wd understand.*

while nevada finds a nurtured protection from the same phenomenon:

*mama/ will he be handsome & strong/ maybe from memphis/
an old family of freedmen/ one of them reconstruction senators
for a great grandfather. . .*

their particular distortions interfere with them receiving one another
as full persons:

claire
no no/ i want nevada to understand that i understand that sean's a
niggah/ & that's why he's never gonna be great or whatever you
call it/ cuz he's a niggah & niggahs cant be nothin.

nevada
see/ earl/ she's totally claimed by her station/ she cant imagine
anyone growing thru the prison of poverty to become someone
like sean

claire
sean aint nothin but a niggah nevada/ i didnt know you liked
niggahs.

such is the havoc created in the souls of people who arent supposed to
exist. the malevolence/ the deceit/ & manipulation exhibited by
these five are simply reflections of the larger world they inhabit/ but
do not participate in:

sean
contours of life unnoticed/

michael
unrealized & suspect . . . our form is one of a bludgeoned
thing/ wrapped in rhinestones & gauze/ blood almost sparklin/
a wildness lurks always . . .

oppression/makes us love one another badly/ makes
our breathing
mangled/ while i am desperately trying to clear the air/
in the absence of extreme elegance/
madness can set right in like
a burnin gauloise on japanese silk.
though highly cultured/
even the silk must ask
how to burn up discreetly.

3/21/80 NYC

takin a solo/
a poetic possibility/
a poetic imperative

if i asked: is this james brown or clifford jordan? you wd know. if i
said: is this fletcher henderson's band or the blackbyrds. you wd
know. i say. pick one: ayler or coltrane. here's another: charlie parker
or ben webster. most of you wd know. the tone. the lyric. rhythm &
cadence of the musician is a personal thing to you. you listen & learn
the particular flow of a particular somebody.

soon you'll say that's oliver lake. not julius hemphill. or that cdnt be
david murray. that's gotta be hamiett bluitt. you cd go so far as to say
joseph jarman wd never play anything like that. or even point ornette
coleman out/ shd you see him in any where/ & say . . . he is history.

we can do this with any kinda horn . . . clarinets, saxophones,
trumpets/ tell me what does 'some day my prince will come'/ mean
to you. that is not snow white or walt disney/ that is miles davis.
some of us can even differentiate mongo santamaria from pablo
'potato' valdes and ray barretto from pacheco. others can pick ron
carter from a segue of mingus & hopkins & favors. we hear so well/
remember solos that were improvisations/ we are thoroughly smitten
by the nature of the thing/ if we talk abt music.

you never doubt bessie smith's voice. i cd not say to you/ that's chaka
khan singin 'empty bed blues.' not cuz chaka khan cant sing empty
bed blues/ but cuz bessie smith sounds a certain way. her way. if tina
turner stood right here next to me & simply said 'yes' . . . we wd all
know/ no matter how much i love her/ no matter what kinda wig-
hat i decide to wear/ my 'yes' will never be tina's 'yes.' and that's
what i want to discuss with you this evening.

we, as a people, or as a literary cult, or a literary culture/ have not
demanded singularity from our writers. we cd all sound the same.
come from the same region. be the same gender. born the same year.
& though none of the above is true, a black writer can get away with/

abscond & covet for him or herself/ the richness of his or her person/ long before a black musician or singer cd.

now why is this? we don't understand the beauty of language? that cant be true. according to dillard & smith we make up a good part of contemporary american/ on our own/ cd it be?/ we assume a collaboration with any blk writer/ who attempts to recreate blk english/ blk culture/ cuz that's ours/ we were there/ we know abt that/ & that poet/ that novelist/ that playwright/ happened to be there at the time/ when some other somebody, just like me/ waz sayin or doin/ exactly what i say & do/ that wd mean there is absolutely no acceptance of blk personal reality/ that if you are 17, female & black in the u.s.a./ you have one solitary voice/ though you number 3 million/ no nuance exists for you/ you have been sequestered in the monolith/ the common denominator as persona. what i am trying to get to is the notion that as a people we have so claimed 'the word'/ we dont even pay attention to who is speakin. is this leroi jones:

> who will know what I am and what I wanted
> beneath the maze of memorys & attitudes that
> shape the reality of everything. Beneath the
> necessity of talking or the necessity for being angry
> and beneath the actual core of life we make
> reference to digging deep into some young woman,
> and listening to her come.

or imamu baraka?

> we do not need to be fucked with
> we can be quiet and think and love the silence
> we need to look at trees more closely
> we need to listen

there's a difference/ in syntax, imagery & rhythm & theme. who is this: bob kaufman, david henderson? or thulani or papoleto melendez or me:

> i seek a phone & let you have it
> what you see is what you get
> if you limit yrself — you lose

that's the division of a realm bordered by bebop & one sunk in syllable/ where only the language defines reality. we have poets who speak to you of elephants & avenues/ we have others who address themselves to worlds having no existence beyond the word. that's fine. we live all those places. but, if, as i believe, we dont know the voice of a writer/ the way we know 'oh . . . that's trane'/ something is very wrong. we are unfortunately/ sellin ourselves down the river again. now/ we awready know abt that/ if we go down river again/ just cuz we don't know or care to recognize our particularities/ wont nobody come/ cuz dont nobody care/ if you dont know yr poets as well as yr tenor horns.

you dont resist count basie cuz he's from red bank, new jersey . . . i never heard of any one disparaging eric dolphy for bein born & raised in los angelos/ nobody is mad at pacheco cuz he is from the dominican republic/ but i can tell you who is a poet from chicago/ i cd say that's some west coast stuff/ or some new york number/ & there will be a great noddin of heads & huh-huns/ cuz we dont ask a poet to speak/ we want a poet to talk like an arena/ or like a fire station/ to be everywhere/ all at once/ even if we never been there/ but especially/ if we've never been there/ we expect a poet to clear a space/ not her space/ not a secret/ not a close room/ but the town/ we assume the poet to be the voice of everywhere we are not/ as opposed to bein 'everything we are' . . . though what authentic musical criticism of our artists that exists/ always allows them the space to be themselves. A. B. Spellman did not write a book callt/ bebop. he wrote a book called / four lives in the bebop business/ in black music/ leroi jones demanded only that each apple core/ be singular/ be, in this case, himself/ though that had more to do with circumstance than sexism.

my basic premise is that poets address themselves to the same issues as musicians/ but that we give the musicians more space to run with/ more personal legitimacy than we give our writers: here is a series of poems & compositions that approach the same themes/ if not the same themes they approach the same energy levels/ if not the same energy levels/ they approach the same rhythmic offensive: as/ sun ra's version of *take the a train* / ishmael reed:

> *i am a cowboy in the boat of ra*
> *vamoosed from the temple i bedded*
> *down with Isis, Lady of the Boogaloo, dove*
> *down deep in her horny stuck up her Wells*
> *Far-ago in daring midday get away.*
> *'start grabbing the blue'*
> *i said from atop my double (crown)⸮*

or take victor hernandez cruz' *doing poetry*:

> *the poet sees & hears the world. & there are many*
>   *worlds.*
> *people live in different worlds/ got different bags*
> *humans talk/ dance & make noise/ a poet must*
>   *make poetry*

> *out of that/ or make poetry out of his mind/ which*
> *took form in the world*
> *words ☞ music travel.*
> *god wd not make anything bad or dirty. some people*
> *make dirty things happen tho.*
> *i see what's in the world ☞ sing it like a god.*

& give the rest to dolphy . . . there is no incongruence, here. but you wd know dolphy & maybe not hernandez cruz. here/ compare leroi jones with himself as Baraka:

> *seeing no one. not wanting anyone. but you all.*
> *i want now to have all your minds. want now, to be*
> *them.*

here is another nuance of baraka: *beautiful black women:*

> *Beautiful black women, fail, they act, Stop them,*
> *raining.*
> *they are so beautiful, we want them with us. Stop*
> *them raining*
> *Beautiful, stop raining, they fail. We fail them ☞*
> *their lips stick out perpetually, at our weakness.*
> *Raining. Stop them.*
> *Black queens, Ruby Dee weeps at the window,*
> *raining, being lost in her life,*
> *being what we all will be, sentimental*
> *bitter frustrated, deprived of her fullest light.*
> *Beautiful black women, it is still raining in this*
> *terrible land.*

as so often assumed by academicians, the work as leroi jones does not overshadow the work of imamu technically. now/ hear david murray's *flowers for albert* & know that sorrows or incantations may be as gentle as they are grieving/ as lyrical as they are abandoned to despair:

here, clarence major: *reflex ☞ (bone?) structure:*

> *on the wall is an edward hopper painting of an*
> *all-night*
> *diner. the loneliness kills me. they bury me*
> *in atlanta.*
> *core invited shirley mac laine ☞ marcello*
> *mastroianni to the funeral but they dont show. a lot*
> *of colored writers send flowers.*

imagine adrienne kennedy's opening speech in *rat's mask* with albert ayler's *ghosts:* (brother rat)

kay within our room I see our dying baby, Nazis
screaming girls & cursing boys, empty swings, a
dark sun. there are worms in the attic beams. they
scream and say we are damned. i see dying and grey
cats walking. kay within our room i see a dying
baby, Nazis, again they scream and saw we are
damned. within our once capital i see us dying.

here is gylan kain's *love song number 33* which fits perfectly with
julius hemphill's *hard blues:*

we make love in the burning tenement
my knife
upon yr womb
fingers upon yr neck/ you scream
black satin woman
you are the boston strangler turned in upon yr self
i am not the man who kicked you
down the endless shaft of stairs
i am the black flute
yr vulva lips refused to play.

or compare bob kaufman's *song of the broken giraffe* with oliver
lake's *altoviolin* or roscoe mitchell's *nonah:*

I continued to love despite all the traffic light
    difficulties
In most cases, a sane hermit will beat a good
    big man
we waited in vain for the forest fire, but the bus
    waz late
all night we baked the government into a big
    mud pie.
Not one century passed without Shakespeare calling
    us dirty names
with all those syllables, we cdnt write a cheerful
    death notice.
The man said we cd have a birthday party, if we
    surrendered.
Their soldiers refused to wear evening gowns on
    guard duty
those men in the basement were former
    breakfast food salesmen
we hadda choice of fantasies, but naturally we
    were greedy . . .
at the moment of truth we were dancing a minuet
    & missed out.

Kaufman's voice is quite like muhal richard abrams' *1 & 4 plus 2 & 7.* we assume the tune or the composition is the person/ is the reality the tune is/ we assume a poet has no grounding/ the poem can float in the air & belong to all of us so long as we deny the individuality of the word/ the specificity of language cd allow us so much more. i suggest that thulani davis is quite as inclusive as the art ensemble of chicago/ in *people in sorrow:*

> *with closed lips & knotted secrets/ choke*
> *   the speech/*
> *cut the throat/ cut the throat behind the veil*
> *the rich phantasma. wanted not taken*
> *the nightmare & the dream*
> *if you ask for me/ i'm never there*
> *i hide in the streets*

until we believe in the singularity of our persons/ our spaces, language & therefore craft, will not be nurtured consciously/ our writers will come across it/ if they want. but we wont recognize it/ cuz like i said is that (conyus?)/

> *the way of the new world is endless, imposing*
> *   & present*
> *there is a different reality that i cannot recognize*
> *in the living nor dead; the earth is moist with them*
> *& below the vastness of the backwater*
> *lie drummed skinned boys collapsed in silence.*

or jessica hagedorn?

> *sometimes you remind me of lady day*
> *& i tell you sadness*
> *the weariness in yr eyes/ the walk you have*
> *kinda brave when you swing yr hips*
> *sometimes serenity in yr eyes*
> *& the love always.*

i know you know the difference tween elvin jones & tony williams? if you take us as seriously as you take a saxophone, maybe we'll have decades of poems you'll never forget.

we assume a musical solo is a personal statement/ we think the poet is speakin for the world/ there's something wrong there, a writer's first commitment is to the piece itself. how the words fall & leap/ or if they dawdle & sit down fannin themselves. writers are dealing with language, not politics. that comes later. so much later. to think abt the politics of a poem before we think abt the poem is to put what is correct before the moment/ if the moment waz not correct/ it still

waz/ we dont castigate ornette coleman for 'lonely woman' nor do
we chastise the del-vikings for singing abt love all the time/ we accept
what they gave us/ cuz that's what they had & it waz good.

when i take my voice into a poem or a story/ i am trying desperately
to give you that/ i am not trying to give you a history of my family/
the struggle of black people all over the world or the fight goin on
upstairs tween susie & matt/ i am giving you a moment/ like
something that isnt coming back/ a something particularly itself/
like an alto solo in december in nashville in 1937.

as we demand to be heard/ we want you to hear us. we come to you
the way leroi jenkins comes or cecil taylor/ or b. b. king. we come to
you alone/ in the theater/ in the story/ & the poem/ like with billie
holiday or betty carter/ we shd give you a moment that cannot be re-
created, a specificity that cannot be confused/ our language shd let
you know who's talkin, what we're talkin abt & how we cant stop
saying this to you. some urgency accompany the text. something
important is going on. we are speakin. reachin for yr person/
we cannot hold it/ we dont wanna sell it/ we give you ourselves/
if you listen/

thulani:

> *yes the holy ghost waz fine tonight*
> *but i had to leave him in the place*
> *you see i just walked in off the street*
> *& i'm trying to keep a date*
> *i'm tyring to give away what's left of me*
> *that aint been bought or just plain taken*
> *y'know i try so hard to keep ma biziness to myself*

if you listen/

pietri:

> *we are gathered here today to say we are gathered*
> *here today because we are not gathered somewhere*
> *else to say we are gathered here today & not*
> *somewhere else we are gathered here today because*
> *this is somewhere else/ & because we are not*
> *gathered somewhere else to tell you differently.*

if you listen/

Kaufman:

> *jazz—listen to it at yr own risk*
> *at the beginning, a warm dark place*
> *(her screams were trumpet's laughter*
> *not quite blues, but almost sinful*
> *crying above the pain, we forgave ourselves)*

you cd imagine us like music & make us yrs.

> *we can be quiet & think & love the silence*
> *we need to look at trees more closely*
> *we need to listen.*

How I Moved Anna Fierling To The Southwest Territories

or
my personal victory over
the armies of western civilization

one evening last winter as i cut & pasted the preliminary script of
spell #7 in the lobby of the Public Theater i noticed a great bustling &
repressed hysteria in the air. i saw more white men than usual in
tuxedoes & three-piece suits. there were lavishly clad women of all
types & classes posing by the stairwells & elevators of a building i
worked in. i paid little attention until i saw what i thought waz a
group of official people. in this case, Mr. Papp, Herman Badillo, some
one who i thought waz the mayor, some other people i waz sure were
undercover cops & Gail Merrifield. oh. i said. there is some thing
going on. then i realized that i must be cutting & pasting away, while
Coriolanus prepared to open. well, i said to myself. shd i stop my
own work to go see a classic that has not been altered to fit the needs
of my century or my people? shd i stop work on something i feel so
tenderly & passionately abt in order to submit myself to the presence
of critics who can only hear that Afro-Americans & Latinos have diction that is not the diction of white folks? why shd i do that, i said to
myself, when i can stay here with my own characters who talk fine to
me/ who talk to me abt what i care abt. oh/ i said. Zake. you are an
educated Afro-American. you can't stay away from Shakespeare on
those grounds. you are trained to hear the lyric & wisdom of anything
in the English language/ & Shakespeare/ well you were certainly
exposed to Shakespeare. But an anglophile i am not.
  the compromise. finish the script for *spell #7* that wd make up for
any racial slights or abuses i endured in the audience. out of respect
for the actors & Shakespeare i wd catch the second act & return
another day to see the first act. after all/ i'd read *Coriolanus* when i
waz 15 years old/ there waz no urgency abt all this.
  yet that waznt true at all & i knew it. the urgency existed because
of the vicious racist & virtually colonial attitudes expressed in the
critical responses to Julius Caesar, the first production of the black &
latin Shakespeare company that Mr. Papp had formed in the fall of

1978. not since Governor Faubus & good old George Wallace standing
in the schoolhouse doorway had i read such indictments of the capac-
ity of non-white people.

i had & still grapple with the idea of classics in the lives & arts of
third world people. we have so much to do, so much to unearth abt
our varied realities/ on what grounds do we spend our talents,
hundreds of thousands of dollars, unknown quantities of time, to re-
create experiences that are not our own? does a colonial relationship
to a culture/ in this case Anglo-Saxon imperialism/ produce a sym-
biotic relationship or a parasitic one? if we perform the classics/ giving our culture some leeway in an adaptation/ which is the parasite?
why aren't the talents & perspectives of contemporary third world
artists touted in the same grand fashion successful revivals of dead
white artists are? all these things bothered me during the second act of
Coriolanus but not so much that i waznt moved to tears simply by
the overwhelming power of the company/ i loved looking at them/
hearing them. i waz thoroughly committed to seeing more black,
latin & asian artists addressing issues of the world. one thing that
doing classics allows us/ that is such a relief/ is to do an evening of
dialogue without having to restrict ourselves to the pains & myopia of
racism in America. the power of white folks as we know it poses no
boundaries in *Coriolanus* or *Julius Caesar*. they are not in it and hold
no power—what escapism. the failure of the black & latin Shakespeare
company is directly related to the actual power of white folks & the
impotence that that sort of power brings. this impotence is an inability
on the part of white audiences, critics, academicians & their specific
mythologies of white supremacy to identify with black and latin characters and to accept black & latin actors as nobility. for in our hemisphere race & class are implacably engaged & it is a duel to the death.
it resulted in the death of the black & latin Shakespeare company.

i cd feel as i clapped & shouted during curtain calls that it waz
only the black folks who were clapping & shouting. the white people
in the audience seemed more amazed that the black people had
understood Shakespeare/ or that it waz possible to enjoy an entire
evening when not a nigger danced/ let alone sang. I waz filled with an
uncomfortable blend of excitement abt the actors, disdain for the
audience, anger that we had to do this at all, & satisfaction that we
had. i went to have a drink, to think, to talk to somebody abt the
mess of my fortune to be born black & English-speaking.

at Lady Astor's i waited for the actors to congratulate them i
thought/ or to commiserate/ cuz Ira Aldridge had done this 200 years
before. cuz waznt *Native Son* a classic/ cuz there waz nothing to
combat the irrationality of racism that assaulted such benign adapta-
tions as *Carmen Jones, The Wiz, & Medea*. I waz angry/ for didnt i
have a right to see my own kind do whatever in the hell they liked? if i

had to struggle to identify with Anna Karenina & Blanche Dubois/
why cdnt white folks learn that skill/ that great leap of imagination
that lets another person of another color become oneself. i began to
list all the 'white' shows i shd have seen done by black people/ so the
experience cd have been more personal/ not fraught with so many
double thinks & excuses. i began with Twain/ *Tom Sawyer &*
Huckleberry Finn. the list grew to include *Cat on a Hot Tin Roof,*
Death of a Salesman, Marat/Sade & *Mother Courage.*

Oz Scott, the only director with whom i had worked at that time,
came to pick up the script of *spell #7*. i realized that what i feared abt
the classics had indeed happened to me. i had forgotten abt my own
work & waz involved in fruitless combat with myself abt the works
of dead white men. just what white folks want. the only recourse waz
to quiet the antagonisms i waz experiencing/ once & for all. how? by
making the demon (the classics) bend to my will. only by directly
assaulting what i felt as an oppressive authority figure wd i free myself
of the need to continually debate what i really understood to be a
waste of my time & energy. cuz my own life history revealed that no
matter what i thought i waz doing the public perception had to do
with that i waz a black person & what a miracle it must be for me to
be articulate.

Oz & i decided on *Mother Courage*. this waz an arbitrary decision
based on mild intoxication & Brecht's more aristocratic position in
the company of Twain, O'Neill, & Miller. we delighted in the obvious
presumptuousness of two black people assigning themselves the task
of toying with one of Europe's precious sons. i went around Lady
Astor's with Oz speaking to actors, black & white abt my sudden
respect for the classics & how all black people really must do one/ it's
like having one's pedigree verified. some weeks later/ with no instiga-
tion from me/ Mr. Papp called to ask if i wd consider adapting
Mother Courage. yes. i said without hesitation. now i wd move what
waz sacred to them/ to something sacred for me. manipulation of
symbols is not unlike big game hunting. learning the habits, expec-
tations & reflexes of other animals allows us to slay them. i wd have
my chance to hunt the cherished words of dead white men & using all
my Afro-American reservoirs of magic, hate, & understanding of my
people/ undo one myth & replace it with my own.

while i've never been fond of anglophone literature, i've always
respected german writers. i dont know why. my guess is that i move
toward that which is contrary to the traditions of the language that i
learned to hate myself in/ as a black person/ as part of the colonial
bounty of empires built from the sweat of my particular ancestors.
with all the fallacies rampant in that thought (think of Martinique,
Curaçao, Brazil), my penchant for German & French literature exists
to this day. doing *Mother Courage* wd permit me to pay homage & to

defeat the prophecies of Bertolt Brecht/ who i admired immensely at
the same time that i cd never trust cuz/ he waz after all still/ white:
my admiration for Brecht is in the text of my adaptation and the care i
took not to betray him. but if a work is truly classic it must function
for other poeple in other times. i believe that Brecht's work does this.
his love of the complexity of ordinary people/ his commitment to a
better life for all of us/ his use of politics & passion/ music & mono-
logues/ were not so different from my own approaches to the theater.
(i might have felt estranged had Mr. Papp asked me to adapt Chekov,
Artaud, or O'Neill.) i also knew that Brecht had much more artistic
control of his work than i wd have of my adaptation. first because i cd
not direct such a massive piece. second, because i had no Paul Dessau
or Kurt Weill of my own to produce the sounds of the Reconstruction
as i heard them. in this way, my Brechtian adaptation waz inordin-
ately non-Brechtian. nevertheless, the text left me plenty of room to
exert my powers.

   Mother Courage has most to do/ at least from my vantage point/
with the actual responsibilities all of us must accept for the machina-
tions of the capitalist state. the history of Afro-Americans is so mired
in the sluggish imaginations of racism that our true experiences in the
development of this country are looked upon as quirks. how in the
hell cd the 14 million blacks freed after the Civil War have an insigni-
ficant relationship to Manifest Destiny, to miscegenation, the
franchise, the life of a nation moved by dreams of empire & subjuga-
tion of nature from sea to shining sea? that's where my *Mother
Courage* begins/ with the first thirty years of struggle by the first
mass of freed slaves to become American. the first thirty years of our
culpability in the genocidal activities of the cavalry, the exploitation
of non-English speaking peoples, the acceptance of the primacy of the
dollar. if i must come to terms with being a descendant of imperialist
assimilationists who were willing if not eager to murder & destroy
other people of color, in the name of a flag that represents only white
folks, then let me use a vehicle conceived in the heartland of one of
history's most cruel ideologies, Nazism. being Afro-American does
not excuse our participation in the hoax of the myths of the western
pioneers. nor does the fact that we are black disavow the courage of
those pioneers who were willing to fight the land, their better judg-
ment & the never-ending viciousness of racists with no more than
Jesus & a shotgun.

   i now have no further need to experience intimately the thought
processes of a great white dead writer/ in the way i lived Brecht's conscious mind for six months. *Mother Courage* gave me the opportunity to ground myself in the history of my people in this land. i can
offer this version of Brecht's masterpiece as the adventures & trials of
people of color of the last century in a language of my own. now i

have colored wagon trains & towns, black conquistadores & hood-
lums, wenches & ladies of refinement embedded in the soils & myths
i waz raised on, but excluded from. i have no need to deride or defend
the social experiment of third world companies dedicated to the
classics/ i have resolved the conflicts for myself. i owe not one more
moment of thought to the status of European masters. i don't have to
worry that Ira Aldridge thinks poorly of me for not accepting a chal-
lenge/ the battle is over. i am settling my lands with my characters,
my language, my sense of right & wrong, my sense of time &
rhythm. the rest of my life can go along in relative aesthetic peace/
the enemy has been banished from my horizons. as the magician in
spell # 7 said: " crackers are born with the right to be alive/ i'm
making mine up right here in yr face/ why dontcha go on ahead &
push me."

Movement/Melody/Muscle/ Meaning/McIntyre

Chants that must be sung. Music that must be heard, to pacify spirits, consecrate our souls, we sometimes call magic. Dianne McIntyre calls it dance. Her company, Sounds-in-Motion, is such a force that we must repent, rethink, reinvent, remember all our lives cause it's urgent. And we're strong. No matter how the 20th century has denigrated the human body, the black people, the land, McIntyre's choreography insists that living is arduous and remarkable. Her suites, *Life's Force* (1979) and *Shadows* (1975), push the dancers till we cannot believe they could move again. Another leg cannot extend. Who could leap? Where is breath for a contraction more? How is it possible? And that is McIntyre's point. Human energy is infinite. We can do more. We must. Even her own solo, *Triptych* (1980), in collaboration with Max Roach and Abbey Lincoln, was an unrelenting assault on her body. Her innate lyricism sustaining her, grace under pressure, a city dweller's rosary.

McIntyre's pieces are the legacy of millions of Americans who are here because their forebears did what they had to do. Their lives depended on it. That's how McIntyre's Sounds-in-Motion performs her work: Like if they don't do these dances, they might die. At the Symphony Space, February 7, McIntyre resurrected *Memories* (1975) and *Union* (1974). These are dissimilar pieces requiring different skills and approaches from the dancers, as well as challenging their resourcefulness to make an old dance new. The core of the group, Bernadine Jennings, Lonetta Gaines, Mickey Davidson, Fred Davis, Ahmed Abdullah, and Babafumi Akunyun, has been with McIntyre since the mid '70s.

I first saw *Memories* in 1974 at the Henry Street Settlement House. Since that time McIntyre's work has become more complex spatially and rhythmically, moving toward sculpted impulse and labyrinthine density. Yet *Memories* highlights certain basic McIntyre aesthetics: reliance on popular Afro-American dance; respect for Afro-

American music; and a sense of the conceptual realities available to us through these forms. It is not that McIntyre's work rejects folklore, but her versions of what is folkloric are formed by the here and now. There are no accidental ethnic references. It is all on purpose.

By the time the regal Lonetta Gaines as The Woman in *Memories* has settled in her chair and quieted, we know that this black woman is a particular history. She conjures visions of special moments she has to remember or acquiesce to numbness. Eubie Blake's early compositions with Noble Sissle propel her visitors, Her Mother and Her Father, portrayed by Gwendolyn Nelson-Fleming and Fred Davis. Nelson-Fleming's return to Sounds-in-Motion after a long absence is gratifying. Her full body and light feet remind us that dance is not restricted to those slight of limb.

The parents' "couple-dancing," in all its sexuality and fun, is how The Woman remembers them. These characters are not Puritan America. They are black America, facile, sensual, and hopeful, as evidenced by McIntyre's solo as With Hopes. Bernadine Jennings's presence, With Despair, elicits wonder at the length of her legs and the reach of her eyes. Sashaying with her battered broom, Jennings's body rejects pity, succumbs to the fatigue a cleaning woman must know, and startles to an innocent joie de vivre if she steals a moment to dream. Mickey Davidson, With Love, beguiles with the precision of her movements, the tenacity of her body. Coupled with Phillip Bond, Young Man, there are allusions to Ailey's *Fix Me Jesus* duet from *Revelations*.

Memories is a rare McIntyre composition in that it is linear. There is a narrative line drawing separate elements into our view. From this point on, as demonstrated in *Union*, the only lines McIntyre's concerned with are geometric emotional architectures, personal landscapes created with the bodies of her dancers. McIntyre hankers for flat repeating horizontals, punctuated by suspended contracted torsos, rectangular leaps, arched turns, and squared hips. McIntyre shapes territories for her dancers. They are not exiles. They are not without a place where they are in control.

The South African horizons evoked by Ahmed Abdullah's trumpet ease Jennings across the floor. Akunyun's brilliant percussion pushes Bond, Davis, and Brown off the ground explosively. Muneer's cello, positioned like an electric bass, tosses Davidson, Banks, and Gaines off center toward flexed images: craters, torn fences, skyscrapers in a quake. Gwendolyn Nelson-Fleming's voice rides over it all like the wind, a siren, a mother's wail. The musicians of Sounds-in-Motion give credence to the possibilities of old-fashioned call and response in a modern American dance company.

That McIntyre includes the verse of Langston Hughes and Margaret Walker doesn't mean her dance is not saying something she wanted to say. Rather, McIntyre assumes responsibility for accurate

41

portrayals of our history: letting who said it first take credit, take part in the continuing struggle. This is why there is no end to *Union*. The company is literally flying, cutting the air, as the lights fade. The music goes on. Our lives depend on our coming together. While we breathe, there can be no bows. There is no rest.

The Harlem Cultural Council's persistent efforts to present contemporary choreographers is paying off. Had it not been for the Dancemobile Winter Series, McIntyre might not ever have reconstructed *Memories* or *Union*. We would not have had the opprotunity to see her consistently vigorous use of the black female body—Jennings, Gaines, and Davidson belie the notion that strong women are masculine. We are primordial energies: molten, direct, irrepressible. Just watch a Jennings stride. Her extensions could push laser beams out of her way. Gaines's arms embrace parallel dimensions that her legs intersect. Davidson's energy rushes through her fingers so that her body is electric.

McIntyre's commitment to improvisation, so that her dancers make their own statements within the rubrics of sound and sweat, is the foundation of a company that does not lie. When Sounds-in-Motion moves, they mean it. Our lives depend on this.

Did I Hear the
Congregation Say Amen

. . . I'll play something and she takes it and runs. She is one of the great black singers in the tradition of all the other great singers . . . the black woman who's dealing with the new music. She does not back off. —Andrew Cyrille

Jean Lee does not need a band. She does not need to tell us to come to her. She does not need a microphone or electricity. There is nothing an elevator could do for Jean Lee. She sings, sometimes with the Galaxy Dream Band and sometimes on her own. But she sings. Did I hear the congregation say Amen.

At Soundscape a couple of weeks ago, Jean Lee performed "The Poem As Song/The Song As Ritual." On 52nd Street I realized Jean Lee is clothed and fed by her voice. That's the same street my aunts and uncles were born and black on, so 52nd and 10th means something to me—like a people who come out with what they can carry: love, sweat, blood and song. Though everything we know is wonderful and rich, we, as a people, hide, to keep it safe. Jean Lee don't. Jean Lee didn't hide behind her dancers or her musicians though it would have been easy, with the likes of Andrew Cyrille on drums and percussion, Gunter Hampel on vibes, bass clarinet, flute, and piano, Thomas Keyserling on alto sax and flute, William Parker on bass, and Rrata Christine Jones's dance.

Aretha addresses God. Billie Holiday seduced him. Tina Turner made the devil think twice/but Jean Lee is mingling among us.

Just take a stroll down Seventh Avenue
and tip your hat
to ev'ryone you meet.
You see the world
on Seventh Avenue;
it's in the eye of ev'ryone you meet.
Just tip your hat,

43

your heart,
your soul,
your feet,
and greet the world
in ev'ry 'I' you meet . . .
Say, "how are you,
and you, and you
and you. How do you do,"
ya do ya do ya
do . . . (improv.)

—Jean Lee, Wellspring

She is not afraid of all this body that moves so sweet I dare
you/and isn't this more than you ever imagined; her body is song.
Moses as a child would have flown on his bed of rushes had she been
singing by the Nile.

"why you call the moon
His majesty?"
"well baby,
the moon is like a man, to me;
doin' all his fine
little tricks and show
with the clouds,
and then comes beamin' out
so proud
and sure
of himself.
For me,
the sun is a woman;
round
and warm
and
life giving.
Maybe they're each
a little bit of both."
Amen.
"You got it baby."
mmmmmm-Lawd!
I'm so HAPPY 'bout dis child."

—Jean Lee, Conversations

It is such a relief to meet a wild black woman and live where she lives among those she has chosen. Now we could visit at home listening and sharing her records. The collaborations with Jimmy Lyons and Andrew Cyrille, Nuba (Black Saint), or the remarkable *Blase* (Byg) with Archie Shepp, but then we could have Ms. Lee all to ourselves on her own record *Conspiracy* (Earthforms). If we still can't get enough, there is always the Lee-Hampel discography to explore. *Journey to the Song Within* (Birth), *Enfant Terrible* (Birth), and *Out from Under* (Birth) have never left me wanting.

Her voice is full like Chaka Khan's, or soft like young Gloria Lynne. There is the ache of an Etta James, sometimes, the heights of Minnie Ripperton before she knew pain. Makeba's insolence as well as the sensual hush of Leci Brandao slip in. From time to time, it's just/Jean Lee.

It is enough to say I heard about Mahalia. My grandma told me 'bout Clara Ward. But I saw Jean Lee. Maybe there are too many of us with too much need/so we *have* to not sing. We have to listen for the Word. Lee leads us up and out of Cyrille's percussive melodies, through the swinging Chicago spaces Rrata C. Jones creates. Well. Did the congregation say Amen.

Jean Lee can't talk unless she moves, and one thought would not occur without the other. Here we've got a tradition who could be like Dinga McCannon and Chase-Ribaud's sculptures, flowing in space. We got a woman among us who isn't afraid of the sound of her own voice. She might lay up nights, wondering how are we staying alive 'cause we didn't hear what she just heard/or sing it. Well. Did I hear the congregation say Amen.

She sings.

Jean Lee/She sings.

Voice, April 29–May 5, 1981.

Black Dance America, Brooklyn Academy of Music, April 21–24, 1983

A Celebration of Black Survival

Journal Entry #692

what does it mean that blk folks cd sing n dance?
why do we say that so much/we dont know what we mean/
i saw what that means/good god/did i see/like i cda
waked on the water myself/i cda clothed the naked & fed
the hungry/with what dance i saw tonite/i don't mean dance
i mean a closer walk with thee/a race thru swamps that fall
off in space/i mean i saw the black people move the ground
& set stars beneath they feet/so what's this mean that
black folks cd dance/well/how abt a woman like dyane harvey
*   who can make*
her body the night riders & the runaways/the children hangin
on they mama's dress/while they father's beat to death/the
blood/from de man's wounds/his woman's tears/the night riders
goin off in darkness/the silence of the night
how abt bernadine j. whose body waz all of that in 5 min-
utes/& whose very presence humbled all but the drum/
now that's a dance/like rael lamb careenin cross
the stage on his bare stomach/fifty feet/
sounds like possums n rattlesnakes/mississippi undercurrents
& steamin hog maws/tossin him from decatur to south texas/
tearin him from contraction to leaps so expansive/his body
took the space allowed thirty redwood trees/&those sounds
kept pushin him/little racing motors like the cops waz
round the bend/windows opened & shut cuz there are things
others ought not hear/feet on stairways of burned out homes/
the sounds pushed him/& there was a dance that was a black
dance/that's what it means that black folks cd dance/it
dont mean we got rhythm/it dont mean the slop or the hully gully/
or this dance in houston callt "the white boy"/it dont mean just

*what we do all the time/it's how we remember what cannot be said/
that's why the white folks say it aint got no form/what was the form
of slavery/what was the form of jim crow/& how in the hell
wd they know. . .*

N. Shange, *Sassafrass, Cypress & Indigo*, 1982. St. Martin's Press

What do we mean by this racist cliché that all black folks can sing and
dance? Some answers were provided by Dance Black America, April
21 through 24, 1983, at the Brooklyn Academy of Music. The Festival
afforded us an intellectual as well as aesthetic immersion in the
realms of Afro-American movement since the Diaspora, also known
as slavery. Colloquia examining regional and folk dance, the legacy
and implications of Dunham, our relationships to Latin and African
forms were preparations for performances and choreographic
exploration by Afro-Americans from all over the country.

Many of these movers I have seen before.

In the basement of a church in Harlem, Chuck Davis teaches till
sweat seeps from the floor and the spirits of the drums push ancient
Africa from our modern black bodies. On East 12 Street in New York
City, Rod Rodgers is free in movement and committed through dance
to the end of racism, nuclear war, and hunger. Uptown at Sounds-in-
Motion on Lenox Avenue, Dianne McIntyre utilizes what we know of
Cunningham, Horton and Graham with the force of her slight body:
herself, dance. Downtown Eleo Pomare in his dances addresses
muscle and the patient strength that has kept Afro-Americans in the
New World from disappearing from the face of the earth. His *Las
Desenamorados* is more than a realization of the pain of being "the
unbeloved." It is a singular effort to find the believable in the midst of
despair: the impossible.

Chuck Davis's *Lenjen-Go Mandiani*, Rod Rodgers's *Box*, Dianne
McIntyre's *Etude in Free*—only part of this marvelous distillation of
our struggle to survive: Dance Black America.

Donny McKayle's *Rainbow* is one gift my mother gave me; his
lyricism is still "una regala," a gift. *Road of the Phoebe Snow*, Talley
Beatty's contribution to the program, is one of the more technically
difficult pieces of our time. I saw it performed admirably, courageously,
by the Alvin Ailey Repertory Ensemble. Blondell Cummings performed her *Chicken Soup*, in which the kitchen is the center of our
lives. Once in San Francisco, she and I planted fifty-five bulbs of
flowers, to bloom as black dance in America should bloom. We are a
blossoming people, "flora negras." Louis Johnson once stopped me on
Grove Street to say we must dance. His *Forces of Rhythm*, performed
impeccably the the Philadelphia Dance Company, fuses classical,
modern, ethnic, and jazz styles, showing us how to dance, and why.

We must sing and dance or we shall die an inert, motionless, "sin ritmo" death. "Negros muertos," killed by a culture afraid of who we are and what we have to say with our bodies, our music, and our brains. Black folks do have brains. We even have ideologists, scholars, choreographers, and always the grace of the gods . . . although my teacher, Fred Benjamin, sometimes tests Christ, inviting Mary Magdalene to pick up her skirts and switch a bit to the beat of her soul: our souls—a collective whole. One poeple, one motion in myriad forms. Ask Vévé Clark, the dance scholar, what she does in Haiti. I assure you, bad back or not, she's not reading books. She's dancing. Between the legendary feet of Pepsi Bethel and the jazz of us all, between Charles Moore and "el afro-latino de nosotros," there is a space open to all human beings unafraid of the ferocity of a people who take dance seriously, who seriously dance, and are generous enough to share.

Such as *Lenjen-Go Mandiani*, performed by the Chuck Davis Dance Company.

Listen to the drum from Congo Square to East 110. Lift those feet! Swing those arms! Become a swan who sees something she can't resist up in the sky somewhere. Church Davis lifts us off our feet. A scenario, life uptown moving to the beat. What beat? "Say, man, where's the party at? Right there under your feet!" in the words of Time, the slick-headed boys from Minnesota. Chuck Davis demonstrates it, brightly.

Lots of critics only talk about our costumes, our colors. That's true, we are a people of color, with color. We cula ful: yellow, violet, green, orange, pink, and always black. Many rows of women, hips back and forth, east to west; young men in the throes of the drum as we all are, if we feel it. Never forgetting the flexibility of our backs—say our necks, in different circumstances. We sing. We dance. As Vévé Clark said at one the festival's symposia, the question is not "what is black dance," but "What it is." Dance on. Pat those feet through the soil. Let those toes grip the earth we worked. Take back the land, the souls of our great-grandparents in the earth. We don't need no shoes. We need to dig and jump into the land we come from; one woman after another, one dream upon the other, calling up who we are. If there are still questions about the angers of Afro-American dance, look only at the bent knees, fluid backs, vigorous arms of the Chuck Davis Dance Company. "No hay nada mas de discutar." Such as Arthur Hall's *Marie Laveaux and Danse Congo Square*, performed by Arthur Hall's Afro-American Ensemble:

Through a remarkable golden raffia emerge dancers as slaves, looking for a moment to, as Larry Graham says, "puleese release yourself." In this piece the European influence of the New World is already apparent in the "danzon" nature of the movement and the coupling off of male and female. At that time we were merely property with rhythm. In Curaçao, Martinique, Vera Cruz, and Charleston we danced these dances, a strange syncretism of "las Siete Potencias" the Seven Powers, and for what we had become in the New World, manifest in the walk of Arthur Hall.

The excerpt from Hall's *Fat Tuesday,* a high ceremony of candles, sequins, and drums, with a deity draped in yellow and black, undulating under marvels of feathers, takes us back once again to some form of parity. A movement not defiled, or at least not violated, though we all know the truth of the matter. In West Africa, Elégua was a young man, virile guard of the crossroads. In the New World, Elégua is an old and crippled man. Think for a moment: Our cross-road was an ocean. Double-dutch to sand-dancing, roller discos to Lucume, alive and well in Cuba. There is always a continuity to our movement, Subtle, erotic, informed by history, known and unknown.

"Hambone, Hambone, have you heard." Seven young men stomp out, letting us know that the gracious beauty of the disco dances emerges from the crudity and unselfconsciousness of our workers— our ancestors, called slaves. We make minstrelsy our own, even wearing red velvet, but no burnt cork. Our dance reflects the many ways we've avoided death, insisted on living. For the beat, for the heat, for the freedom of dance. Ain't no way to keep us down on no ground; We just jump up again and again and again.

A brass band and saxophones leading us to someone's promised land. An old New Orleans procession, right here in Brooklyn. Like we don't have to go so far to get home. Dejan's Olympia Brass Band of New Orleans can always see me "home" by the mercy of our Lord Jesus Christ, whose cross appears in the sky as the band escorts the lost soul to the Promised Land. Very bright colors, of course, because nothing stops Carnival.

Such as Lenwood Sloan's *Darktown Strutter's Ball/Strut Miss Lizzie,* danced by Halifu Osumare and Leon Jackson, with Neal Tate on the piano and Ruth Brisbane singing:

So black et rouge. We've been everywhere; ask Josephine or Katherine. Our music and dance is our answer to our interaction with the world—all of it, from Clark Air Force Base in Manila to Guantanamo. A black somebody felt something enough to move him/her: "Let's do it, let's do it till we can't stand no mo'."

In Oakland, California at Everybody's Creative Arts Center Halifu Osumare breathes, relaxes. Her movement reflects today and yesterday. Tonight at BAM, in "All The Dusky Gals Were There," Osumare is as enchanting as any Southern belle could be, including Scarlett O'Hara. She and her partner, Leon Jackson, exhibit the delicacy we have managed to sustain throughout the bombing of Tulsa, the riots of Liberty City, and "white only" water fountains. We have a grace

50

about us that Dunham may have called the ability to stretch. We are all ready at the barre. The stretch is survival.

Such as the Navy Yard boys Club Sea Cadets' *Pickin' Em Up and Puttin' Em Down:*

Military grouping. "Cultura y Armas." In case we forgot there's a struggle going on here. In Nicaragua, El Salvador, St. Alban's, Angola —seems like everywhere black folks live, we gotta be ready to fight. Turn about and open ranks in your sunglasses and apple jack caps. Defend our right to make art. 1-2-3-4. Turn to the rear. Cover your back. You are too precious to lose, to abandon here in Brooklyn. Dance on, guns in hand. Who would know which was make-believe, the guns or our spirit? Who would dare take a chance on making a mistake?

Such as *Harlem Rent Party,* an assembly of dances performed by Mama Lu Parks' Jazz Dancers:

Take some tap dancing, a boa or two, and black hips: "now that gonna be a dance." Our bodies become our instruments. No trumpets, but some feet that don't miss a beat, and never missed the "A Train." Shakin', shakin' on up past 59 Street, straight to 125, where we all know what the step is. Especially for a rent party, where we doin "Sweet Georgia Brown." Pick up them feet. Pass the hat. Oh, remember the Apollo amateur nights. Now Mama Lu Parks with a young Sammy Davis tap dancing with a younger Debbie Allen. Time step, triple that, and break-it-on-down. Where'd you put that accent, boy? This is the real deal. Don't mess around 'less you really plannin on 'messin' with it.

In Brazil, we play the dozens with "Capoeira." Here in America, English-speaking, we play the dozens with taps and our tongues. But there's always a winner—an older man, experienced warrior of rhythm like Al Perryman. For without our drums, there's only our hands and feet, the voice of a people supposedly inarticulate, assumed inaudible. But James Brown and Little Anthony never had problems being heard, nor did George Jackson. Silently, moving along like Sojourner in the night, moving on toward liberty.

But right now, we gonna Lindy Hop. Pachucos and black folks living for the moment of glory, when we move. War or no war, what has our life been: one long marathon dance. Pass that hat. The rent's due. Dance it up. Dance it away. Ballet shoes aren't enough to say alla this. Get those feet up off the ground and put them women up in the air. This here's a life dance. It's hard, and full of travail. Get them feet off of the ground. Reach for the world. Take it.

"You Could Have Been Anything You Wanted To," the BISS Harmonizers sing for us, bringing us to our childhoods and recent history of corner du-wop. "Babee, how could I let you get away?" Where did we let black dancers go? Can we find a place in our hearts for all we been missing? Can we get a hold to it now? Who is looking for Sonora Matancera or Celia Cruz? Who is looking for Pepsi Bethel or Sounds-in-Motion? Elijah said we were the lost-found people. Let's find ourselves now. It's in the beat, the beat called destiny.

We could paint our way out like Doze, spray can in hand behind the Jazzy Double Dutch Jumpers, but foreigners call our culture that graffiti. Fab 5 Freddy says we can rap our way out, but the foreigners call that illiterate. What is the path to freedom, and how many ways can we get there? Dance on. Rap on. "Don't Stop 'Til You Get Enough." Smurf on, brothers. Just don't hurt yourself, man. Be a little more gentle on them black bones. Listen to Master Blaster. He say, "It's called survival. Only the strong can survive." And it's true, black folks do sing, and glory hallelujah, we do dance. Dance we do.

Dance Magazine, September, 1983.

A Weekend in Austin:
A Poet, the People, and the KKK

Austin Texas
2 febrero 1983
Congress & Third Street
"Out of El Salvador"
"Money for Jobs
Not Guns"
"I'm from Puerto Rico."
"Que Viva Cuba Libre
Que Viva La FMLN
Que Viva Puerto Rico Libre"

It was too late/ how the ol' folks say
it was *too* late by 7:00 a.m.
to stop the sheets of fog
dense & wet/ encompassing
lakes & souls/ alla Austin
too late by mid-mornin' to stop

Death To The Klan
they comin' in trucks/ jeeps/ n things
high noon/ west texas
in a fog
we can *barely* see/ thru
hardly move in/ we slow
motion marauders/ ravagin'
these sheets/ these ol' ol' sheets
savannahs blancas
sangre y las marcas de neustra historia

**"Damn The Klan
&
The Capitalist Hand
Behind It"**
*"Yo soy trabajadora sola y
feminista"*

*Strong brown woman, what my folks
call a 'stirdy gal',
in a red T-shirt*
    "By any means necessary"
*malcolm's face now/ listen to me
wanted dead or alive in tejas
like Gregorio Cortez*

She's a working mother with a
"hard workin' husban' ". They've got
four children here in Austin. This
fine lady's in a *pink* jacket/ her red shirt
emblazoned with a map of
Africa/ 'continuous struggle'/ neath
Malcolm's face/ of course.
la lucha continua/ ain't it, though.

**"El Pueblo Unida Jamas
Sera Vencido"**
An adolescent in PLO headdress,
a *'hatah'*: "The KKK is equiva-
lent to the Zionist assassins.
*"Yo soy Mexicana en solidaridad
con la gente de Palestina y Mexico"*

**"Black Brown Yellow White
Oppressed People Must Unite"**
Hands clap like the boots of the
Sandinistas at the Bank of America,
Managua, Nicaragua/ Julio 19, 1979
La Victoria
in Austin
we just walkin' . . . we ain't doin' nothin'
but walkin'

"Defend The People"
"I'm from Algeria. I joined the
March cause I don't like the Klan.

I feel, here, among people of same
color. We're all joining together
against oppression, especially, the KKK.
We heard a lot about the Klan
in Algeria."

"Abajo Con El Klan"
A smallish young *gringa* with her
guapo negro and their child of
18 months are moving slowly; the
baby is in a stroller. The
husband says: "Equality should
be for everybody. That's what America's
founded on. My daughter, Salima (her
name means peace), she's here standin' up
for her *own* rights today."

Eyebrows like the night, hair of a raven,
and smiling thru all this pain, a white
feminist almost skips with us. Her shirt
reads, simply, "ESPRIT". *Espiritu.*
Spirit.

Jose Garza is a large Chicano, one you
would expect to find working with
some big herds of cattle years ago.
He is the father of Cuáuhtemoc Garza
who is only 4 months old. Jose empha-
tically explains:

"*Cuáuhtemoc* [Aztec name]
is here because the Klan *must* be stopped.
Cuáuhtemoc is awready *un guerillero.*
We came 75 miles, from San Antonio, *con
nuesto futuro*, Cuáuhtemoc."

Rita Moya *y su hermano*, Rubén Moya,
with his boy, Nicolas of only 7 weeks,
actually marching *como en
Vera Cruz y hay
guitarres.* Rubén says: "Nicolas *esta
aqui porque*, we're family. He must be
enlightened to people and ideas; because our Nicolas *es el futuro.*"

The flag of Free Palestine is carried
with honor of two Palestinians. By the
way, the flag is green and black stripes
with a red triangle where you might put
a fist on the right hand side of Israel.
The one wrapped totally
by his 'hatah', so
he can remain anonymous whispers to me:
"We support anti-racist people and *all*
oppressed people, because we are
oppressed people." We have ta keep movin',
the State Capital is just in fronta us,
say 100 yards fore the 'real deal'.
Got me!

A 19-year-old black girl from Austin
with straightened hair in french braids;
a little preppie jacket & beige slacks
sorta moves to the beat of her soul, while
she tells me: "I'm heah to help get
the Ku Klux Klans outta Heah.
My Mamma ain't heah, on accounta, she
sick. That's the *only* reason she ain't come
today."

**"Reagan & Klan Work
Hand-In-Hand"**
Lines and lines of raised hands: *blancas,
morenas, indias, negras, aziaticas,* our
hands together: *tejanos*/ texans. We
reaching toward the sky/ thru the fog
them sheets of fog. Maybe 'we' the sun/
Forget the weather.

**"We Fired Up
Won't Take It No Mo'
We Fired Up
Won't Take It No Mo.'"**

The speeches begin.
We are blazing.
The sheets & trucks
they stilla comin'
High Noon/ West Texas

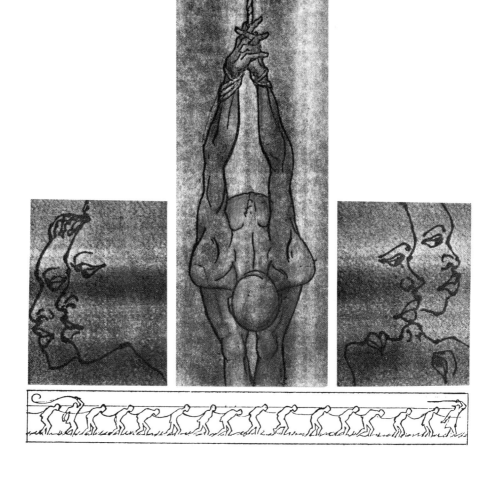

**"We Fired Up/
Won't Take It No Mo'
We Fired Up/Won't Take It
We Fired Up/Won't Take It
We Fired Up/Won't
We Fired Up/**
    fired up/ fired up/ fired up . . ."

The State Capital Building South Wing
Very amiable, blond, muscular Texan,
Mr. Larry Todd,
Public Information Officer, Texas
Department of Public Safety:
"Our role is to insure the safety
of *everybody* here: tourists,
protestors, and our citizens. The troopers
are trying to assist and that's their
responsibility. The police are still
working their beats. The Highway Patrol
is out on the roads. The County Sheriff's
Officers are still out working the rural
areas. By 5:00 p.m. today, I hope
everybody will have their say and go home
without being hurt."

The fog is liftin'
but the sun sho' nuf ain't shinin'
Tom Joad ain't never walked this heah
particular RED RIVER STREET
not this heah pretty one/
by the lakes. in the sheets of fog
Austin/Texas/U.S.A.

**"We Fired Up/
Won't Take It No Mo'
We Fired Up/We Ready To Go"**

Voice, March, 1983.

Palabras y Balas
("Words & Bullets")

Diario Nicaraguense

The New Orleans airport is as French as America can get, I guess. It has none of the gracious surrealism of Orly, nor the grandeur of de Gaulle. In fact, eight American white men meandered all over le Bistro where I was having my preflight white wine. These white men talked only of guns: when they clean them/how they hunt/how their wives are jealous of their guns/& how they are carrying their guns to Nicaragua. Are they going to shoot the Nicaragüense/or me, cause I'm black & in le Bistro/some animals? Who do they think animals are? Would they recognize one? Haven't we died enough awready?

Dear Friends:
I am glad to let you know that groups of hunters of birds of migration are always welcome to our country and this Institute is always willing to help.

Herty Lewites
Ministro, Instituto Nicaragüense de Turismo,
'Año de la Unidad Frenta A La Agresion'
Managua, 12 de Enero de 1982

Quetzal was a bird. Tupac Amaruc was a man. Atahualpa is in exile. El Malecon is a tangible solution, when I dream my child shall know what it is to fly.

Managua, Thinking About Cuba

Dreams of the Malecon haunted me after reading & rereading *Three Trapped Tigers*, Cabrera-Infante's romance with Cuba before the Revolution. A road by the sea, the length of an island, El Malecon.

All of Cuba, a slow walk.

Last June in La Habana with theater people from Uruguay, Nicaragua, Mexico, El Salvador, Colombia, we walked many nights, El Malecon. Rum. Poetry. The full moon. Old women walking their dogs at 4 a.m., safe. Lovers on the sides of El Malecon, safe. The sea rushing toward Cuba as the rest of us should, to feel the weight fall off our backs, nuestras corazones. To breathe in "el primero territorio libre en America." One mohito, *rhum con yerba buena*. Alan showed me his wounds from the struggle against Somoza, talked of his theater, his guerrillos when not in combat. Palabras y balas. Poesiá & dying.

Atahualpa had not seen Sara in 15 years, since "El Galpon" was smuggled out of Uruguay, after torture, after threats, after refusing to be silent. Sara waited hours for his plane from Mexico. Atahualpa, 75, waited 15 years to see the actress he'd "made," or so she said. He, also, said there is no writer who can afford not to be an actor, nor an actor who can afford not to be a writer. There is too much to do.

A Cuba libre. Theater in the factory at 2 a.m. Work first. Make theater where you work. Warm milk. Many hugs. Many kisses. Promises to return. We stand, cheering the victorious Nicaragüense, Daniel Prego & Alan Bolt, who have arrived from "el otro territorio libre en America."

For el Primer Encuentro de Teatristas Latino-Americanos y del Caribe sponsored by Casa de las Americas, June 1981:
Enrique Buenaventura/Poeta de Colombia
¡ *Presente!*
Patricia Ariza/La Candalaria de Colombia
¡ *Presente!*
Eddie Armanda/La Mama de Colombia
¡ *Presente!*
Claudio Bregon/Teatro Nacional de Mexico
¡ *Presente!*
Cesar Vieira/Uniao e Olhio Vivo/Brasil
¡ *Presente!*
Adrian Vargas/Teatro de La Gente/San Jose/California/USA
¡ *Presente!*
Sergio Corrieri/Teatro Escambray/Cuba
¡ *Presente!*
Roberto Armijo/Poeta y Trabajador Cultural Internacional/El Salvador
¡ *Presente!*
Miriam Colon/Puerto Rican Travelling Theater/New York & San Juan
¡ *Presente!*
Carlos Barron/Rodrigo Duarte/Oscar Ciccone/Ronnie Davis/Ntozake Shange Amigos del Teatro de los Estados Unidos
¡ *Presente!*

Everyday. Theater. Theater. Make it work for everybody. Everywhere.
Teatro. Teatro. Teatro. Libre.

Quetzal was a bird. He brought the stars out in the night that we
might know light in the darkness. Quetzal was fed with our blood.
Our liberty still demands *nuestra sangre*. Our blood is our ultimate
offering. In El Salvador we are still bleeding. In Nueva York a two-
month-old baby freezes to death in her crib. Her "blood" never
flowed.

Her spirit could not touch us. She never learned to fly. She never
saw "El Brigadista." She does not know that children in Managua,
Santiago, Soweto, Luanda are saving themselves from hungers for
freedom. She does not know that some children with pistols took on
the world & won.

She'll not see the butterflies Remedios saw. She'll never know
another world.

Managua, Remembering SAHSA #415

All the way from Nettleton, Mississippi, & Corinth, Mississippi,
six white Americans are flying on their own to Honduras to build a
church. They are sponsored by Operation Outreach. I thought they
said Operation Outrage. Then I would have asked them to fix the fur-
naces of the freezing in Chicago, Gary, the Bronx. But Outreach is not
outrage. I am following President Reagan's advice. I am on my way
everywhere there is "opportunity."

I am now in Managua. Here we are too precious to be left alone,
longing for heat, salami, bread, or poetry. *La fuerza morale* has no
ethnic boundaries. The Rio Grande aint nothing but a river. On the
other hand, there are all of us: the rapids, violent, rushing, beautiful.
Atahualpa is in exile. At the airport, my old friend, a poet, Roberto
Vargas, is a Sandinista. We hugged, free of decadence, full of hope/ *la
dignidad*.

Inter-Continental Hotel, Managua

"Nicaragua is a country of poets & volcanoes," Roberto boasts. I
sleep with the windows open. The former Bank of America towering
over Managua. Sandino's silhouette, glistening yellow lights, all upside the sky, all upside the former Bank of America. Roberto says the
lights of Sandino came on for me. One second before I looked, it had
been dark. Quetzal has always had a relationship with the night, with
light. Suns, stars, struggle, siempre.

El Malecon, The Westside Highway, U.S. 1, Rte. 66, our peri-
meters. *Estar,* to be, *ser,* to be. What are we dying for? Simply, to be.

4 DE FEBRERO

Los Antojitos, Managua

i must go to La Costa/on the Atlantic side/where
the English left Nicaragua/black & poor
Carlos Rigby/cherry brown in a afro/keeps us
up in the night under Sandino's light/reading poems/
recovered from the war/small pieces of paper/left
at someone's house/small typed pages that could fit
in his shoe/Somoza JAILED poets
     KILLED poets MAIMED poets.

there is something from the war/still
hurting Carlito's leg/he cannot stand in
line for his lunch/
he reads all night of the black coalminers—gold
miners/choking on dust/racism/having no future
that is not/another black hole in the ground.
carlos reads the poems he can/the rest

were BURNED by friends/when the security police/
la guardia nacional/came looking for a free black/
mind/BURNED poems cannot return/we must
fix Carlito's leg/he must be able to stand up/
when he poets his black black language/the reggae of america libre
the hot side of the new way/the bottom of the future does
have rhythm/el ritmo/

i must remember to remind my poet friends in America to keep/
matches in their houses/i must remember that everywhere
nothing can be taken for granted/
     not yr thoughts. not yr beliefs.
they go with you or you burn them/
behind you/   Crimnal/huh
to watch fire eat love of what you come from/what
you want /Necessary for the children/we can
always remember/but

Anywhere at anytime a Nicaragüense may shout out/
     "Si Nicaragua Venció
     El Salvador Vencerá"
From all quarters the Sandinista is answered/in mass response.

"THE SOVEREIGNTY OF A PEOPLE IS NOT DISCUSSED. IT IS DEFENDED WITH ARMS IN HAND."

SANDINO

in Spanish, of course.

Armies come some place to kill someone. Police come somewhere to kill someone. I have always been among the expendable: the ones who could die & not be missed. In Haiti the secret police come out in their noisy trucks with their 1950s bayonets to keep us from leaving our houses at night/that we might speak of anything. In Argentina police who are not police take, loot, rape as they choose & the police who are police thank them. In North America the police let us terrorize one another, so we are afraid of our own countrymen, as well as the police. In America in 10 years more black men killed each other than died in the Vietnam war. We get afraid of ourselves, our power.

In Nicaragua the EPS, Ejército Popular Sandinista, is us, formerly expendable people taking care of ourselves, not killing each other. All of us, poets, workers, campesinos, doctors, the EPS is all of us, for us. So who should be afraid? Who would rather not be associated with "them," with us?

Ernesto Cardenal is not afraid. In Managua I am not afraid. I am not in danger. My child is. She is still in New York where the police don't always see us & see themselves. Our police aren't poets, so poets die. Martin Perez, Henry Dumas, dead poets. Always on the subway, poets die.

Everyone in Nicaragua can name at least one dead poet. Poets who died before the Revolution. Poets are powerful, idealists, sometimes we change the world. This is no Baudelaire nightmare. No opium with Edgar Allen. These were poets with guns/Leonel Rugama Ricardo Murales Aviles Arlen Siu Felipe Peña Rigoberto Lopez Perez Edwin Castro/not here because Somoza & those like him would rather see us dead. 50,000 others, Nicaraguense, who may have written nothing or everything are also dead/not here.

Galeria Praxis: Exposicion de Pintoras Grabadoras/Juan Rivas

Juan Rivas is 25 years old. His whole life Nicaragua struggled against Somoza. His life has been *la lucha*. Yet his paintings let us know he has known love. The kind of love that B.B. King sings about. The love that don't let you down, when your belly's full with some child & one of Somoza's fools puts electric prods by your vagina. The kinda love possible for the Nicaraguan people whose wounds, keloids, bandages, missing limbs, must be caressed, kisst, made welcome again. Yes, you are still beautiful. The struggle has not made you ugly. So young, to have resolved the beauty we must find in those painful, hideous moments. So young, to paint a woman covered, almost mummified, with bandages. A flower, her vagina opening, a palm leaf.

5 DE FEBRERO

Rafael called from Tegucigalpa again this morning. He cannot understand why I just can't leave from La Costa for Tegucigalpa. "There is so much work to do," he says. I say, "I have to go home. There is so much work to do." How could we have argued about where there is more work & which one of us should be where, doing it? But, we did. I'm going to Tegucigalpa on my way home. Compromise as progress/ or a little romance. There was no time for flirtation, when we met in La Habana. We worked, we danced a revolution. Nothing personal.

El Commandante Tomas, tousled gray hair, heavyset, erect, talks of the insanity, the gall of the U.S.A. to accuse the Nicagüense of killing Indians, of racism. I sit next to a Galil machine gun, an Israeli gift to Somoza, with Ernesto Cardenal & escort, thinking of the hunters from New Orleans. Who are the animals?

Lovers in the military zone, Miguel Bonilla, leave their doors open, sit in their yards naked in the moonlight/the sunlight, listening to Prince or "let's get physical" by you know who. In Leon, where Ruben Dario, the national poet, was born, women nurse their babies next to walls fulla bullet holes. Celia Cruz sings "Usted Abuso" for *Radio Amor*. Dedications flow in: for *mi morena*, for *mi negra linda*,

mi guapa chabala, mi chocolaté linda. The radio skips sometimes,
the mortar holes in the highway.
A painter in the Sandinista Popular Army designs weapons now.
He loves landscapes, La Costa, Grenada, the volcano, Momotombo.
He smiles: "A drawing is a drawing."

6 DE FEBRERO
La Cita Bar

Commandante Nora Astorga is Nicaragua's Vice-Minister of
Foreign Relations. While Somoza was alive, she was a lawyer who
worked with banks. She was active aboveground in the women's
movement against the regime. She is very lovely, pretty. Somoza's
right-hand man took a liking to her. After months of planned encoun-
ters with Perez Vega, one of the most hated of Samoza's familiars,
Nora invited him to her house for a "drink."
It was March 8, International Women's Day, 1978, when "Perro
Vego (Dog Vega) relaxed in Norita's home. Norita sent the chauffeur
off for some rum. The FSLN, Frente Sandinista por Liberacíon
Nacional, squadron assigned to her took care of all the rest. Vega's
throat was slit. He was laid to rest: face down, pants down, with an
FSLN flag draped over his body. Norita covered this memorial with
feminist literature.
Days later she sent a communiqué to *La Prensa*, absolving anyone
else of responsibility for the act. This communiqué was accompanied
by a photograph of Norita's daughter/give her a kiss from Nicaragua.
There are the hunters/El Salvador.

8 DE FEBRERO
New York

I almost forgot the chocoyos: lime green/olive green/blue green
birds who fly in the crater of the volcano at Masaya. They follow the
steam & light. They've always survived, always been beautiful.
Always, the eruptions, the lava, the red glow.
The U.S. Customs officials in New Orleans admired the hunters'
rifles, had a good ol' time. I had to empty my pockets. Identify
Excedrin P.M. But then I didn't go to Nicaragua to kill animals. How
did I know there was a poetry festival in Nicaragua? Why did I go?
Who sponsored my trip? Was I employed by anyone? Had I been to
Nicaragua before? How did I get to Nicaragua, anyway?
They did not ask me if I wanted my daughter to know how to fly.
They did not ask about Amalita, the muchachita, whose face is a warp of

scars from Somoza's bombs. They did not braid her hair. They didn't ask if she had eaten or who fed her. She'll be a poet. She told me that. She follows painters & sculptors in the nights. Watches them in the day. She knows there is a world beyond Bloomingdale's, where Nicaragüense still fly to shop: there are our dreams/our children/ what you cannot bomb or buy: poets & volcanoes, the children.

con la Revolución hubo sangre y sacrificio, pero también hay
    musica, teatro, poesiá, y danza
El Commandante Omar Cabeza Lacayo, Jefe del Ministerio
    del Interior
La Barricada, *8 de febero de 1982*

Dance Nicaragua. Dance, in green if you must. In the mountains if you must. Chocoyos with machetes. Chocoyos with machine guns. Chocoyos in the volcano.

Ntozake Shange is a playwright, poet and novelist. Her plays include *for colored girls who have considered suicide/ when the rainbow is enuf, Spell No. 7, A Photograph: Lovers in Motion, Boogie Woogie Landscapes,* and an adaptation of Bertolt Brecht's *Mother Courage and Her Children.* Her books of poems include *nappy edges* and *Daughter's Geography.* Her first and recent novel is *Sassafrass, Cypress & Indigo.* Ms. Shange currently teaches at the University of Houston.

Tom Feelings has been the illustrator of a number of award winning books which include *To Be A Slave* by Julius Lester (Newberry Honor Book, 1969), *Jambo Means Hello: Swahili Alphabet Book* (Caldecott Honor Book, 1975), and most recently, *Something On My Mind,* written by Nikki Grimes (Coretta Scott King Award and ALA Notable Book Award, 1978). Mr. Feelings resides in New York City. Currently he is working on paintings for his new book on the history of slavery entitled, *The Middle Passage.*

Titles from Momo's Press

DANGEROUS MUSIC by Jessica Hagedorn *(poetry)* $4.95 paper.
PET FOOD AND TROPICAL APPARITIONS by Jessica Hagedorn *(novella, stories, & poems)* $5.95 paper, $15 cloth.
BY LINGUAL WHOLES by Victor Hernàndez Cruz *(poems)* $5.95 paper, $15 cloth.
LORCA/BLACKBURN Poems of Federico Garcia Lorca chosen and translated by Paul Blackburn $4.95 paper.
THIS PASSOVER OR THE NEXT I WILL NEVER BE IN JERUSALEM by Hilton Obenzinger *(stories, poems, and interviews)* $5.95 paper, $12.50 cloth.
THE WELLSPRINGS by Harry Lewis *(poems)* $5.95 paper, $12.50 cloth.
THE POETRY READING: A CONTEMPORARY COMPENDIUM ON LANGUAGE & PERFORMANCE edited by Stephen Vincent & Ellen Zweig *(essays from 55 contributors)* $9.95 paper, $25 cloth.

Prepaid Orders will be fulfilled directly.
Please write: **Momo's Press**, *45 Sheridan Street,
San Francisco, CA 94103.*

Book Design by Jon Goodchild/Triad.
Cover photograph by Ntozake Shange.
Backcover photograph by Gregory Gerran.
Drawings by Tom Feelings. Text preparation,
selection and edit by Stephen Vincent, Paul
Cohen, and Beverly Dahlen. Phototypeset
in Trump Medieval by Sara Schrom
at Type By Design, Fairfax,
California.